Buzzy
and the
REDROCK
canyons

Written By Melissa C. Marsted Illustrated By Izzy Greer

Buzzy and the Red

Rock Canyons is written by

Melissa C. Marsted and illustrated by

Izzy Greer. Published by: Lucky Penny Publishing,

LLC, 1776 Park Avenue ❧ Suite 4-369, Park City, Utah

84060-5148. ❧ For inquiries or more information email us at

info@luckypennypress.com or visit www.luckypennypress.com to

see more titles. ❧ Text and Illustrations Copyright © 2016 by Lucky

Penny Publishing. ❧ No part of this publication may be reproduced, stored

in a retrieval system, or transmitted in any form or by any means, mechanical,

photocopying, recording, or otherwise without written permission from

the publisher. ❧ Cover and Book Design by Pamela Beverly-Quigley of Beverly

Design Studio, Park City, Utah. ❧   beverlydesignstudio@gmail.com

❧ Typefaces used are Blend Caps   Engraved ❧ Blend Ornaments

by Typesense, Canvas Script by   Yellow Design Studio, & Futura.

❧ ❧ ❧ ❧ ❧
ISBN: 978-0-615-29588-6

A portion of the sales of our National Parks for Kids (series) will benefit the National Parks Conservation Association.

The Mighty Five® is a registered trademark owned by the Utah Office of Tourism. All Rights Reserved.

"Wilderness is not a luxury but a necessity

of the human spirit."

Edward Abbey

"To be whole. To be complete. Wildness reminds us

what it means to be human, what we are connected to

rather than what we are separate from."

Terry Tempest Williams

THE BEEHIVE STATE

· · · · · · · · · ·

"Welcome to Utah, the Beehive State. I'm Buzzy. I'm going to take you on a journey through The Mighty Five® national parks. You will learn about some of the geology that makes up the rock formations and canyons. Off we go to meet my friends!"

ARCHES
National Park
· · · · · · · · ·

"Here we are in Arches National Park, home of over 2,000 sandstone arches. Sandstone is a kind of colorful rock created from tiny grains of sand or quartz.

"The arches were formed many, many years ago by the weather like rain, freezing cold temperatures and ice. Arches are only counted in the park if they measure at least three feet across. This is Landscape Arch. It is longer than a football field," said Buzzy.

"Hello Miss Magpie!"

"You are one of my favorite birds in all of Utah with your sparkling feathers and long tail! You are such a delight to watch when you fly and swoop in for a landing. You are also very clever! Would you like to explore Arches National Park with us?" Buzzy asked.

"Sure, I would be honored to join you! Together we can learn about and listen to nature's messages," Miss. Magpie said.

"Let's go and find my friend, Mr. Mule Deer," said Buzzy.

"Hello
Mr. Mule Deer."

"How is your day going?" asked Buzzy.

"I was grazing for nuts and berries in these bushes. How do you like my antlers?" asked Mr. Mule Deer.

"They are fabulous and make you look so regal. They must be quite heavy on your head."

"Every year I shed my antlers. Then it will be much easier for me to walk around until I grow new ones."

"Mr. Mule Deer, your character reminds us to be kind and gentle. Just like words might hurt your friends, weather can quickly destroy the canyons and arches. Let's head to my favorite spot in Arches National Park."

DELICATE ARCH

. . . .

"We are at Delicate Arch. It is made of sandstone and is 65 feet tall, as tall as 20 mule deer on top of each other. The person who discovers a new arch gets to name the arch. Some of the arches' names are Parade of Elephants, Double Arch, Broken Arch and Park Avenue Arch.

"Delicate Arch was formed by wind and rain hundreds of years ago. All of the rock formations in the national parks are always changing.

"On we go to our second national park, Canyonlands!"

CANYONLANDS
National Park

· · · · · · · · ·

"Here we are in the area known as Island in the Sky. The rushing waters of the Colorado River formed the canyons and buttes in this national park," said Buzzy.

"What is a butte, Buzzy?" asked Miss Magpie.

"Miss Magpie, thank you for asking questions. A butte is a hill or mountain rising upwards from the land around it. I will take you and Mr. Mule Deer to see the Aztec Butte and then you will both understand."

"See that behind me?"

"That is a granary built into the side of the butte. The ancestral Puebloan people would climb up to the top of the butte to collect food and store it in protected places like those granaries.

"The top layer of a butte is a hardened layer of rock that does not wear away from the actions of wind and weather. Animals cannot hide very well because trees do not often grow in the rocks. Sometimes a seed, possibly dropped by a passing bird, will find a place where there is some soil and will grow.

"Look who's joined us. Mr. Desert Cottontail," said Buzzy.

"Well, hello Mr. Desert Cottontail."

"How do you like living here in Canyonlands?" asked Buzzy.

"I love to rest in the shade of shrubs or under the juniper trees. I also find holes or burrows to hide from the sun or other animals."

"What is your favorite thing to eat?" asked Buzzy again.

"I like to eat plants and grasses," said Mr. Desert Cottontail.

"I hear you are a very fast runner, too," said Buzzy.

"Oh yes, I am very sneaky, too. Instead of being afraid, I zigzag across the desert to escape from other animals."

NEWSPAPER ROCK

• • • • • • • • • • •

"Look what we have here. This is Newspaper Rock with hundreds of ancient rock carvings called petroglyphs. The Native American people drew them over 2,000 years ago. The artists created the drawings of animals, people and patterns with a sharp tool. They removed the top layer, called desert varnish, to show the lighter rock underneath the surface.

"One more stop to visit in Canyonlands. Follow me," said Buzzy.

"We made it to Needles!"

"The area is made of many colorful sandstone spires. A spire is like a tower, soaring high into the sky. It is shaped by the weather. Birds and spires help to raise our heads with confidence. Do you agree, my friends?" asked Buzzy.

The three answered together, "Yes, of course! We can do anything we set our minds to do!"

"This is one of my favorite spots to rest in Canyonlands after a long flight."

"The juniper tree is one of the strongest trees in all of the national parks. The tree roots are especially hardy. Even when they are knocked over by wind, junipers grow, but very slowly. Their twisted tree trunks have a magical and enchanting quality about them.

"I love to land on a branch and catch my breath and enjoy the views," said Miss Magpie.

"I hope you enjoyed our adventure through Arches and Canyonlands. I'm flying across the state to my next stop, Capitol Reef National Park. Thanks for joining me. See you soon," said Buzzy.

CAPITOL REEF
National Park

· · · · · · · · · ·

"Welcome to Capitol Reef National Park. Here, we will see hundreds of canyons, towers, and arches and a spectacular line of white domes and cliffs made of Navajo sandstone.

"I will introduce you to some of my other friends, too. Let's go!" said Buzzy.

"Well, hello Ms. Marmot."

"How are you doing on this fine day?" asked Buzzy.

"Hi, Buzzy! I am doing great and enjoying the views from this spot, which is not too high. I came out of my burrow to get some sun on my face and a little something to eat. I have to make sure I am full when wintertime comes and then I will hibernate all winter long."

"What are you planning to have for lunch?" asked Buzzy.

"I am in the mood for some berries and maybe some pieces of grass and moss."

THE CASTLE

· · · · · · · · · · ·

"We are at the Castle, one of the most impressive rock formations in all of Capitol Reef! It is a desert landscape where pinon, juniper and cottonwood trees grow.

"The colors of the rocks and cliffs are very different than our first two national parks, but that is what makes Capitol Reef so fascinating. Look who's climbing there! Mr. Bighorn Sheep. I will ask him to join us on our journey through Bryce Canyon and Zion National Parks," said Buzzy.

"Hi, there, Mr. Bighorn Sheep."

"Your horns are quite large. Why are they so big?" asked Buzzy.

"I use them to defend myself and only the rams, or the male sheep, have horns like I do. We prefer not to use our horns, though. We would rather use our grace and kindness to solve our problems."

"That is very good advice, too. I sometimes sting, or I can be sweet like the cactus flowers I get my nectar from. Will you join us on our travels?" asked Buzzy.

"For sure! I can climb very high up on these steep rocks, almost as high as you can fly," said Mr. Bighorn Sheep.

BRYCE CANYON
National Park

· · · · · · · · · ·

"Welcome to Bryce Canyon National Park!
It became a national park in 1928, almost
one hundred years ago. There are many
kinds of animals living here. We will meet a
Peregrine falcon. One of the most amazing
times of day to visit Bryce is at sunrise or
sunset. There is a steep trail to hike from the
rim down into the massive amphitheater. I
can zip in and out of all of the hoodoos that
make up Bryce Canyon."

"What is an amphitheater, Buzzy?" asked
Mr. Desert Cottontail.

"You can look below and see how there is
a very large space formed in a circle and
that is what we call an amphitheater," said
Buzzy.

33

THOR'S HAMMER

· · · · · · · · ·

"Some of the most famous formations in all of the parks are the hoodoos at Bryce Canyon. The weather and the changes in temperatures at night crack the rocks, and then pieces break away from the tops of the arches to form the hoodoos. Here is one of the most magical formations of all. It is called Thor's Hammer.

"Thor is a name from mythology that means the thunder god. It also represents strength, loyalty and protection."

"Look up there. I see a Peregrine falcon. Do you see him?" asked Buzzy.

"We do!"

"Well, hello, Mr. Peregrine Falcon."

"How do you like your post where you can see over all of the canyons?" Buzzy asked again.

"I love it up here where I can land when I get tired from flying and, then I can hunt from here for my dinner. I like to eat smaller birds that have already stuffed themselves with seeds."

"My friends, the birds soar high into the sky. Looking at them teaches us to raise our heads with confidence. Now let's head back to the rim and wait for the sun to set," said Buzzy.

"One of my favorite times here in the park is when all of the humans have gone and the stars start to fill up the sky. Because the lights from the big cities are far away, we can see many more stars. As the sky gets darker, we'll get to see the Milky Way and Orion's Belt and watch for a falling star to make a wish," said Buzzy.

"Wow, look up there! The Milky Way!"

"That's the constellation Orion, known as the hunter, with three bright stars lined up in a row. Those three stars are known as Orion's Belt. There, over there. Look quickly before it's gone, a falling star. Hurry! Make a wish!" said Buzzy.

"I did it!" said Mr. Desert Cottontail.

"I made one, too!" said Ms. Marmot.

"Tomorrow we will visit our final destination on this trip, Zion National Park. Good night for now!" said Buzzy.

ZION
National Park
· · · · · · · · · ·

"Welcome to Zion National Park! Even though this is our last stop, Zion was Utah's first national park, in 1919. These inspiring desert sand dunes formed the 2,000 foot cliffs many years ago. Rock layers were uplifted, tilted, and eroded by weather conditions that created the colorful cliffs you see here.

"We will get to meet two endangered species while you are with me, too," said Buzzy.

"There they are! Two Mexican spotted owls!"

"They are an endangered species. If we don't protect them while they live in our national parks then they might not be around for others to see in the years to come. They roost in the trees or on the ledges of cliffs during the day and hunt when the sun goes down," said Buzzy.

"They are so adorable with their fluffy feathers!" exclaimed Ms. Marmot.

"Let's go in search of another endangered species in Zion, the California condor," said Buzzy.

COURT OF THE PATRIARCHS

· · · · · · · · · ·

"Look up! The raging waters of the Virgin River created these massive rock formations and cliffs. Hundreds of different birds fly among the canyon walls. If we are lucky we will see a condor. They are one of the largest birds in all of our country. They have a wingspan from the tip of one wing to the other that is nine and a half feet across. Condors are scavengers and eat food that has been left behind by humans or other animals," said Buzzy.

"Look, look! Way up there. I see a condor soaring in the currents of the wind! Today IS our lucky day!" said Mr. Bighorn Sheep.

KOLOB ARCH

• • • • • • • • • •

"This is Kolob Arch. You are fortunate that I am taking you to this hidden gem. It is difficult to find but you will notice that the arch looks like the wings of a condor," said Buzzy.

"Wow, that is truly beautiful! I have never seen such a sight!" said Mr. Desert Cottontail.

"That's why I made this our last stop. Magic is everywhere, in the sky, in the canyons and all around us," said Buzzy.

"I hope you have enjoyed our journey through Utah's national parks. You have opened your eyes and your hearts to the wonders of nature. I will see you next time as we explore other places! Bye for now, my friends," said Buzzy.

"Good Bye!"

About Lucky Penny Press

Lucky Penny Press, a division of Lucky Penny Publishing, is a children's eBook and print publishing company. Lucky Penny Press publishes books written by both adults and children with some of our books published in multiple languages including Spanish, French, and Chinese and with audio recordings.

All of the books advocate messages and lessons that focus on nurturing the creative spirit, introducing new cultures, and empowering children to believe in their dreams. Many of the themes of our books focus on stories of adventure, nature, culture, and the environment.

As part of Lucky Penny Press's cultural fabric, each book is connected to a non-profit organization that receives a portion of the proceeds.

Lucky Penny Titles

In Print on Amazon:

*Emily and the Shackleford Horses** By Melissa C. Marsted and Illustrated By Izzy Greer

Letters to Bridgie Written By Mel Bloom and Illustrated By Karen Folsom

*Pablito and the Speckled Bear** By Melissa C. Marsted and Illustrated By Ben Cicatti

The Extraordinary Pony Written and Illustrated By Alana Clumeck

The King's Balloon Written By Melissa C. Marsted and Illustrated By Karen Folsom

The Mellow Yellow Global Umbrella Poems By Sojourner Kincaid Rolle and Illustrated By Karen Folsom

The Scorch of a Skilten (Middle Grade Fantasy Novel) By Nashat Zaman

Unmask Your Story, A Collection of Creative Projects and Essays By Summit County Utah Teens

Lucky Penny Titles con't.

eBooks available on www.luckypennypress.com:

A Mosaic of Poetry for Kids by former Santa Barbara, CA poet laureate emeritus Perie Longo with a potpourri of artists' illustrations

Butterfly Beach* (in English, Spanish, French and Chinese) Written and Illustrated By Polly Caldwell Bookwalter

Imagine That! A Child's Guide to Yoga By Kenneth K. Cohen and Illustrated By Joan Hyme

Maddie Goes to France (in English, Spanish and French) By Ken Jacquin and Illustrated By Mike Terry

Maddy and the Magic Penny (in English and Spanish) By Celeste Turbeville and Illustrated By Angela Zhu

New Life Helper* (A Ghanian story) Written By Peter Bermant and Illustrated By Izzy Greer

Rex the Cat* (in English, Spanish and French) Written By Hilary Doubleday and Illustrated By Marymount of Santa Barbara students

Songs of the Sandman Written By Kenneth K. Cohen and Illustrated By Izzy Greer

Wake Up to Love (in English, Spanish, French, Italian and German) Written and Illustrated By Corinne Humphrey

The Children's Peace Book, Children Around the World Share Their Dreams of Peace in Words and Pictures By Jolene DeLisa

* indicates that an audio recording of the book is available on the Lucky Penny Press website and/or on iTunes.

LUCKY PENNY
PUBLISHING, LLC

1776 Park Avenue, Suite 4-369 | Park City, UT 84060-5148
info@luckypennypress.com | www.luckypennypress.com

About the Illustrator

Izzy Greer is an artist living in San Francisco, California. She has previously lived in Massachusetts and Utah and has visited all five national parks in Utah on numerous occasions. She has been painting for most of her life, and studied history and art at Williams College. Izzy has been working with Lucky Penny Publishing as an illustrator for over six years. This is her fourth book with Lucky Penny Press.

photo credit:
Jennifer Denton
Photography

About the Designer

Pamela Beverly-Quigley is a designer and creative director with an MFA from the University of Colorado—Boulder. Her design work has included branding and logo development, coffee table books, interiors and more. She has launched large scale programs sold in mass retail and boutiques and has won numerous awards for book and catalog design. Pamela writes about art, design and inspiration on her blog: Patina & Hue at: www.patinaandhue.com. She joined Lucky Penny Publishing in 2015 bringing years of design experience and a love of children's books to our team.

photo credit:
Eric Sullano

About the Author

Melissa C. Marsted is the author of six children's books and the founder of Lucky Penny Press, launched with insurance proceeds after her house and most of her possessions burned in the 2008 Santa Barbara Tea Fire. Today, Lucky Penny Publishing, LLC, has grown to incorporate two imprints—Lucky Penny Press, publishing books for children; and Silver Dollar Press, publishing autobiographies, memoirs, and nonfiction. An endurance athlete, Marsted has completed 12 marathons, including one along the Inca Trail to Machu Picchu in Peru, where she was inspired to write the children's book *Pablito and the Speckled Bear*.

A graduate of Harvard University, with a degree in Classical Greek and an M.A. from Antioch University, Marsted now lives in Park City, Utah. She serves on the Summit County Library Board and is a member of Leadership Park City and the entrepreneurship incubator, Pando Labs. Marsted has two college-aged sons, two cats, and a Jack Russell terrier, Aro.

10 Fun Facts
About The National Parks

1. The world's first national park, Yellowstone, was created in 1872 by President Ulysses S. Grant and it now covers three states, Montana, Wyoming and Idaho.

2. Congress passed and President Woodrow Wilson signed the National Park Service Act establishing the national park system in 1916.

3. There are 59 national parks in the National Park Service, covering 51 million acres about the size of the state of Kansas. Only one state does not have a national park and it happens to be our country's first state, Delaware.

4. California has the most national parks with nine, followed by Alaska with eight, Utah with five and Colorado with four.

5. California also has the national park located at the lowest elevation, Death Valley National Park at 282 feet below sea level. It is only 75 miles away from the highest point in the 48 continental states, Mount Whitney at 14,505 feet high.

6. Crater Lake National Park in Oregon is the deepest lake in the United States.

7. Yellowstone National Park is known for an active volcano called a super volcano which last erupted more than 640,000 years ago. Yellowstone also has thousands of petrified trees and nearly 300 waterfalls.

8. The tallest tree in the world is known as the Hyperion Tree and is located in California's Redwoods National Park. It is six stories taller than the Statue of Liberty.

9. The highest point of all of the national parks is Mount McKinley, rising 20,320 feet. It is in Denali National Park in Alaska.

10. The newest national park is California's Pinnacles National Park which became the 59th national park in 2013.

Made in the USA
San Bernardino, CA
22 October 2016